THIS CANDLEWICK BOOK BELONGS TO:

_____

_____

_____

_____

Once wolves roamed nearly all
the lands of the northern hemisphere.
But they have been hunted and killed
by humans for centuries, and today they
are extinct or very rare in places where
lots of people live, including Europe
and much of North America.

Most wolves now live in the far north
of the world — in Alaska, Siberia, and
parts of Canada, such as the Yukon
Territory, where this story is set.

For John, my North Star J. H.

For William and Daniel S. F.-D.

First U.S. paperback edition 2002

The Library of Congress has cataloged the hardcover edition as follows:

Howker, Janni.
Walk with a wolf / Janni Howker ; illustrated by Sarah Fox-Davies. — 1st U.S. ed.
p.   cm.
Summary: After a lone hungry wolf finds companions whose combined strength drags down
an old moose, the entire pack sleeps through a blizzard and dreams of the return of spring.
ISBN 0-7636-0319-8 (hardcover)
1. Wolves—Juvenile fiction. [1. Wolves—Fiction.] I. Fox-Davies, Sarah, ill. II. Title.
PZ10.3 H832 Wal   1998
[E]—dc21   97-7769

ISBN 0-7636-1872-1 (paperback)

2 4 6 8 10 9 7 5 3

Printed in Hong Kong

This book was typeset in Weiss and Sanvito.
The illustrations were done in watercolor and pencil.

Candlewick Press
2067 Massachusetts Avenue
Cambridge, Massachusetts 02140

visit us at www.candlewick.com

Walk with a WOLF

Janni Howker

illustrated by

Sarah Fox-Davies

CANDLEWICK PRESS
CAMBRIDGE, MASSACHUSETTS

Walk with a wolf in the cold air before sunrise.
She moves, quiet as mist,

　　between spruce trees and birches.

A silent gray shadow, she slides between boulders

and trots over blue pebbles to the edge of the lake.

She plunges through slush ice and laps the chill water,

snaps at a feather that drifts down from a goose wing,

then splashes to shore and

shakes herself like a dog.

Wolves were probably the first large animals to live with people,
and all the kinds of dogs we know today are descended from them.

There's deep snow on the mountains.

Snow clouds bank in the east.

Winter is coming, and the geese fly south.

Run with a wolf as she bounds up the steep slope.

She sniffs at a skull that stares at the lake.

Moss grows on the antlers.

The bone has turned gray,

there's no meat on it now—

and she's hungry.

During the summer months, a wolf may hunt alone
and catch fish, hare, squirrel, and other small animals.
But these creatures go into hiding in winter
to escape from the freezing cold weather.

Howl with a wolf in the dawn, thin and icy.

Deep from her chest the eerie sound comes.

Long, low music.

The song of the Arctic.

Another howl answers.

13

With a wag of her tail, the wolf runs to the pack.

Three sons and a daughter, cubs from the spring,

squirm on their bellies and lick at her neck.

Mother wolves give birth in springtime.
They can have anywhere from one to eleven cubs each year.

14

Although they don't stay together all the time, most wolves live in family groups called packs.

The black wolf greets her with a stare from his pale eyes.

He's her mate, the pack's strongest hunter —

and he's hungry, too.

15

The wolf pack is ready.

They set off together, like eight ghost dogs,

silent and stealthy as the coming of frost.

Three ravens are flying high overhead.

Most packs have up to eight wolves in them,
although packs of as many as fifty have sometimes been seen.

Hunt with a wolf on the trail of a bull moose,

following its tracks and

its scent on the ground.

Wolves have to hunt as a pack
if they are to kill large animals,
such as moose and deer.

There's a crash in the bushes—the moose is close.

The wolves crouch on their bellies,

    their hearts beating fast.

There's danger in hunting—

a kick from a moose can break a wolf's ribs.

Charge with a wolf!

The pack breaks through the bushes,

swift as gray lightning with one bolt of black.

The moose turns and sees them.

But he's old and he's limping.

There are scars on his legs.

The wolves leap at him, biting.

Hear the moose bellow.

Hear the wolves panting as they drag him down.

Drops of his blood fall like berries to the ground.

Rest with a wolf. No longer hungry,

she watches the cubs come to join in the feast.

If there is plenty of food around, pack members will all feed at once.

But if meat is scarce, the strongest wolves will eat first —

and the youngest, the cubs, last.

25

Sleep with a wolf while a blizzard is blowing.

The sky is full of a million gray ice moths,

as the wind drives the flakes down.

Backs to the gale, the wolves curl among boulders,

heads tucked between hind legs,

and noses covered by the fur of their tails.

Dream with a wolf as the North Star is shining.

There's thick snow on the ground and a shivering wind.

But the wolf dreams she is walking

with new cubs in warm sunlight,

as the wild geese return with the spring to the lake.

Index

Look up the pages
to find out about all these wolf things.
Don't forget to look at both kinds of
words — this kind and *this kind*.

JANNI HOWKER is fascinated by wolves. A resident of the United Kingdom, she observes, "The fact that wolves have been extinct here for two hundred years should make me feel safe, but instead it makes me sad. The sound of wolves howling would make winter evenings magical." She is the author of many award-winning books for children, including *Badger on the Barge and Other Stories, The Nature of the Beast, Isaac Campion,* and *The Topiary Garden,* illustrated by Anthony Browne.

SARAH FOX-DAVIES hopes that *Walk with a Wolf* will show readers that "wolves are not the monsters of folklore. They are wild animals that survive only through their skill as hunters and their cooperation as a pack." She is the acclaimed illustrator of several picture books for children, including *Little Caribou,* for which she also wrote the text, *Bat Loves the Night* by Nicola Davies, *Little Beaver and the Echo* by Amy MacDonald, and *Snow Bears* by Martin Waddell.